THE ULTIMATE BOSTON BRUINS BOOK FOR KIDS AND TEENS

160+ Fun, Surprising, And Educational Stories And Trivia Quizzes About Players And History

John Stevenson

ISBN 9798338505083

Contents

CHAPTER ONE

The Beginning: Boston Bruins Early Years

The Boston Bruins are the oldest National Hockey League (NHL) team in the United States. Founded in 1924, they are one of the "Original Six" NHL teams. The Bruins play in the Atlantic Division. They are one of the best teams there, winning six Stanley Cup championships—one of the highest totals in the NHL!

When the Bruins were created, the team's owner chose the nickname "Bruins." It was because it represented brown bears from classic folk tales. The owner wanted the Bruins to be as fearless and strong as those mighty brown bears!

The Bruins first played in the Boston Arena. It is the world's oldest indoor ice hockey facility which was built in 1909. An important moment happened there on December 1, 1924. On that day, the Bruins won the first-ever NHL game played in the United States.

After three more seasons at the Boston Arena, the Bruins moved to a new stadium, the Boston Garden. On November 20, 1928, the Bruins played their first game at the Garden. Unfortunately, they lost 1-0 to the Montreal Canadiens.

But the rest of the season went much better for the Bruins. They even defeated the New York Rangers to win their first Stanley Cup in 1929!

The very next season, the Bruins continued their unstoppable streak. They had the best-ever regular season winning percentage in NHL history. It is a record that still stands today.

Throughout the 1930s, the Bruins were one of the best teams in the league. They led the NHL five times and won their second Stanley Cup in 1939.

Two years later, in 1941, the Bruins captured their third Stanley Cup. However, this would be their last championship win for 29 years. Although the Bruins made it to the Stanley

Cup Finals in 1953, 1957, and 1958, they lost each time to the Montreal Canadiens.

Then, in 1970, after 29 long years, the Bruins finally broke their Stanley Cup drought! With star players like Bobby Orr, Phil Esposito, and Ed Johnston, the team set dozens of records and celebrated a long-awaited victory.

From the 1970s until 2010, the Bruins fought hard for another Stanley Cup. But, they kept facing many heartbreaking losses along the way. It took them 39 more years to finally lift the Stanley Cup again in 2011.

Since then, the Bruins have been striving to repeat their success.

They came close again in the 2024 playoffs, defeating the Toronto Maple Leafs in the first round. But in the second round, they were eliminated by the Florida Panthers, who went on to win the Stanley Cup.

From their early days as one of the original six NHL teams to becoming multiple Stanley Cup champions, the Boston Bruins have truly earned their place in NHL history.

CHAPTER ONE QUIZ

1. What year were the Boston Bruins founded?

a. 1883

b. 1920

c. 1924

d. 1937

2. Why did the Bruins' owner name the team "Bruins"?

a. It represented brown bears from classic folk tales

b. It represented his favorite color brown

c. It represented Boston's old nickname

d. It represented the owner's middle name

3. What is the name of the Bruins' first arena?

a. Boston Garden

b. Boston Stadium

c. Boston Arena

d. TD Garden

4. In which year did the Bruins win their first Stanley Cup?

a. 1910

b. 1912

c. 1929

d. 1935

5. Which team did the Bruins play against in the 1929 Stanley Cup finals?

a. Buffalo Sabres

b. Tampa Bay Lightning

c. Montreal Canadiens

d. New York Rangers

6. In which year did the Bruins win their second Stanley Cup?

a. 1935

b. 1936

c. 1938

d. 1939

7. Which team defeated the Bruins in the second round of the 2024 playoffs?

a. Florida Panthers

b. St. Louis Blues

c. Tampa Bay Lightning

d. Colorado Avalanche

Quiz Answers

1. 1924 **2.** It represented brown bears from classic folk tales **3.** Boston Arena **4.** 1929 **5.** New York Rangers **6.** 1939 **7.** Florida Panthers

CHAPTER TWO
Famous Rivalries

As the Boston Bruins became one of the most famous NHL teams, many major rivals look to defeat the Bruins every time they meet.

Here are three of the Bruins' fiercest rivals, whose intense matchups have produced some of the most exciting and memorable moments in NHL history.

Toronto Maple Leafs

The rivalry between the Boston Bruins and the Toronto Maple Leafs is one of the most intense in the NHL. Both teams are among the best in the league, making them natural rivals. Every time the Bruins and the Leafs meet, the games are filled with fierce competition and excitement!

This rivalry began many years ago. Both the Bruins and the Leafs are part of the "Original Six," the six oldest teams in the NHL.

They played their first game against each other in the 1924–25 season. From 1924 to 2020, they battled it out in 16 playoff series!

One of the most memorable moments in their rivalry happened during the 2013 Stanley Cup playoffs.

In Game 7, the Bruins made an unbelievable comeback. They went from a 4–1 third-period deficit to defeat the Maple Leafs in overtime. It was a heartbreaking loss for the Leafs as they watched the Bruins celebrate and move on to the next round.

Things calmed down a bit after 2013, but not for long. The Bruins and the Leafs faced each other again in the 2018, 2019, and 2024 Stanley Cup playoffs. And each time, the competition between these two teams became even stronger!

Tampa Bay Lightning

Did you know the Phillies have another big rival besides the Leafs? There's another team that gets the Bruins all fired up - the Tampa Bay Lightning!

That is because both teams also compete in the same Eastern Conference, leading to intense games and Stanley Cup battles.

In recent years, the Tampa Bay Lightning have quietly become the Boston Bruins' biggest rivals. Both teams have super talented forwards, tough defense, and some of the best goaltenders in the league. Every game between them a thrilling showdown!

A big moment in this rivalry happened during the 2018 playoff series. That year, it seemed like every call went against the Bruins. Many Bruins fans were upset with the referees for not calling a penalty. It was clear that Brad Marchand was slashed on a breakaway late in Game 2. In the end, the Lightning defeated the Bruins in five games. Boston fans were left disappointed and fired up.

From that moment on, the games are always exciting whenever the Bruins and Lightning meet on the rink.

Montreal Canadiens

The Montreal Canadiens, also known as the Habs, have been the Bruins' biggest rivals for a long time. It's even considered one of the greatest rivalries in all of sports. But in recent years, the rivalry has cooled down a bit.

It all started on December 8th, 1924, when these two Original Six teams faced off for the first time. Since then, they've had epic regular-season games and unforgettable playoff battles.

In the 1950s, the Habs were at their best. They were winning many championships while the Bruins struggled with losses. But things changed in the 1970s when the Bruins became the stronger team.

Over the years, the Canadiens have not been as strong as they once were, while the Bruins have found more success. This has meant that they haven't faced each other as often as before.

The rivalry between the Bruins and the Habs may not be as fierce as it used to be, but the Canadiens will always be remembered as the Bruins' historic rivals!

CHAPTER TWO QUIZ

1. Which team is the Boston Bruins' historic key rival?

a. Tampa Bay Lightning

b. Toronto Maple Leafs

c. Florida Panthers

d. Montreal Canadiens

2. When did the Bruins-Leafs rivalry begin?

a. 1924

b. 1930

c. 1936

d. 1948

3. What kicked off the Bruins-Lightning rivalry?

a. The Leafs defeated the Bruins at the Stanley Cup finals

b. Both teams play in the same division

c. There is a rivalry between Boston and Tampa

d. The Bruins traded their best players to the Lightning

4. In which year did the Lightning defeat the Bruins in five games at the playoff series?

a. 2015

b. 2016

c. 2017

d. 2018

Quiz Answers

1. Montreal Canadiens **2.** 1924 **3.** Both teams play in the same division and compete for the playoffs **4.** 2018

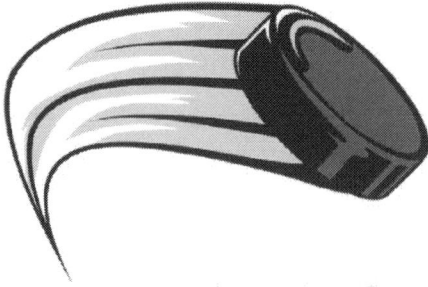

CHAPTER THREE

Legendary Players

The Boston Bruins have some of the greatest players to ever skate onto a rink. Since the beginning of the NHL, the Bruins have produced many Hall of Famers.

These famous Bruins players have shown what it means to play for the Boston Bruins, whether they are winning the Stanley Cup or scoring a point.

BOBBY ORR

**2X STANLEY CUP
(1970, 1972)**

7X NHL ALL-STAR GAMES

8X JAMES NORRIS TROPHY

**3X HART MEMORIAL
TROPHY**

BORN
March 20, 1948
Parry Sound, Ontario,
Canada

SHOOTS
Left

POSITION
Defense

21

"I want that kid to come play for the Bruins," said a scout for the Boston Bruins to his assistant.

From the moment the Boston Bruins noticed 12-year-old Bobby Orr playing in a hockey tournament, they realized that he could one day be a star in the NHL. They wanted to sign him as soon as he was old enough.

When 18-year-old Bobby joined the Boston Bruins, he quickly became noticed for his skill and speed.

He was a defenseman, but he was unlike any other. He could skate like a rocket, always faster than any opponent. He would race down the right wing with the puck, and use his speed and strength to beat the opposing defenceman.

Bobby also had a deadly accurate shot. He could pass the puck to his teammates with accuracy, and score important goals for his team.

As the Bruins started to win more games, they set their sights on the biggest prize in hockey: the Stanley Cup. The last time they qualified for the playoffs was 1959, and they had not won a Stanley Cup since 1941.

Having Bobby gave the team and the fans hope and excitement. And in the 1969-70 season, he would finally bring the Cup home.

That season, the Bruins had one of their best seasons ever. Bobby was leading the league in scoring, and he dazzled everyone with his incredible plays.

But their real challenge was getting to the playoffs. In the first round of the playoffs, the Bruins faced the New York

Rangers. The team played like a unit even though the games were tough. The Bruins won the series and advanced to the next round.

Next, they faced the tough Chicago Blackhawks. It was not an easy series, but again, Bobby led his team to another victory.

Finally, it was the Stanley Cup Finals. The Bruins were up against the St. Louis Blues. This was the first playoff meeting between these two teams.

Every hockey fan in Boston was excited and nervous. Could the Bruins do it this time? Will they finally win the Stanley Cup?

The Bruins proved that they were the better team. They started dominating from the first game, winning 6-1. Bobby was playing like a true NHL superstar. He was making crucial defensive plays while inspiring his teammates.

By the final game, the Bruins were up 3–0 in their series with the St. Louis Blues. But, the score in Game 4 was tied 3–3 after regulation.

The game goes into overtime. Everyone in the arena sat on the edge of their seats. The next goal would end this game and a new winner would be announced. Would it be the Bruins or the Blues?

Suddenly, 40 seconds into overtime, something exciting started happening on the rink.

Bobby passed the puck to his forward, Derek Sanderson, behind the net.

"Over here!" Bobby screamed as he cut to the middle.

Derek sees Bobby and returns the puck.

Bobby collects the puck, beats his defenders, and shoots the puck past Blues goalie Glenn Hall. He scores, and the Boston Bruins win the Stanley Cup!

After the Finals, the streets of Boston were filled with cheering supporters. Bobby had brought the Cup back to Boston after 29 long years.

RAY BOURQUE

1X STANLEY CUP (2001)

19X NHL ALL-STAR GAMES

5X NORRIS TROPHY

BORN
December 28, 1960
Saint-Laurent,
Quebec, Canada

SHOOTS
Left

POSITION
Defense

Ray Bourque is one of the greatest defenders in NHL history. He played for the Boston Bruins for 21 seasons and became a true Bruins legend. He still holds the record for the most goals, assists, and points by a defenseman in NHL history!

From the start, Ray made a huge impact in Boston. He scored a goal in his first game as a rookie in the 1979-80 season.

That year, he won the Calder Memorial Trophy as Rookie of the Year and was also named to the First Team All-Star. It was the first time in NHL history that a rookie, who wasn't a goalie, was selected for the First Team All-Star.

Over his 21 seasons with the Bruins, Ray became an incredible defender. He was so good at reading the game that opposing players found it hard to get past him. He used his stick and body to stop plays and protect his net.

Ray was also strong in offense, which was rare for a defenseman. He could shoot with amazing accuracy and create scoring chances, even from the blue line!

In 1985, Ray became the Bruins' captain and held that role for 15 seasons. It made him one of the longest-serving captains in NHL history. As a leader, he worked hard on the ice and played fair, earning his teammates' and opponents' respect.

One of Ray's most memorable moments came on December 3, 1987. During a special ceremony that only a few people knew about, Ray secretly wore two jerseys. He took off his No. 7 jersey and gave it to Phil Esposito so it could be retired. Underneath, he had on his new No. 77 jersey, which he would wear for the rest of his career.

"Ray, that was a class act out there," Phil Esposito said after the ceremony. "It was an honor, Phil. Your legacy deserves to be remembered," Ray responded sincerely.

Even though Ray achieved many individual honors and set many records, he still dreamed of winning the Stanley Cup. He led the Bruins to many playoff games, but they faced many tough losses.

On March 6, 2000, Ray was traded to the Colorado Avalanche. It was a bittersweet moment for both Ray and the Bruins' fans. He left the only team he had ever played for to chase his dream of winning the Stanley Cup with the Avalanche, who were strong contenders.

"It's tough to leave, but I have to take this chance," Ray told reporters. "Boston will always be in my heart."

Ray finally won the Stanley Cup with the Avalanche in 2001, achieving his lifelong dream. In 2004, he was inducted into the Hockey Hall of Fame. He will always be remembered as one of the greatest legends in hockey history.

PHIL ESPOSITO

2X STANLEY CUP (1970, 1972)

10X NHL ALL-STAR GAMES

5X ART ROSS TROPHY

2X HART MEMORIAL TROPHY

BORN
February 20, 1942
Sault Ste. Marie,
Ontario, Canada

SHOOTS
Left

POSITION
Center

Phil Esposito is one of the greatest goal scorers in NHL history. But, believe it or not, this legendary player didn't make a Junior A team until he was 20 years old!

When Phil was a teenager, he was tall, skinny, and not the best skater. In his first year of playing bantam hockey, Phil didn't make the team. He went home crying because he really wanted to play with his friends.

It wasn't until he was 21 that Phil became a goal-scoring machine. He practiced skating faster, got stronger, and worked hard on his shots.

Phil played his first four NHL seasons with the Chicago Black Hawks. There, he became known as a great playmaker and goal scorer. But in 1967, he was traded to the Boston Bruins, and that's when his career really took off.

When Phil joined the Bruins, he became unstoppable. In 1969, he scored 49 goals—just one goal short of 50, which was a huge number back then. But two years later, in 1971, Phil scored an amazing 76 goals in 78 games. This broke the old record of 58 goals!

Scoring goals was Phil's superpower. Whenever he got the puck near the net, it felt like time slowed down. The goalie would brace himself, trying to guess what Phil would do next, but Phil was always one step ahead.

He waited for the perfect moment and then, BAM! The puck went exactly where he wanted it to.

Phil got really good at scoring goals by practicing at a hockey school in Canada. At the end of each practice, he would line up with all the goalies and grab 10 pucks.

"Okay, get ready! Tell me when you're set," Phil would say to the goalies.

It didn't matter how big the goalies were or where they stood in the net. As soon as they were ready, Phil would shoot —and nine out of ten pucks would go straight into the net.

Phil left the Bruins for the New York Rangers in 1975. By then, he had won two Stanley Cup championships and scored more than 50 goals in five different seasons.

Phil was so great that he was elected to the Hockey Hall of Fame in 1984. And on December 3, 1987, the Boston Bruins retired his famous #7 jersey. He is forever remembered as one of the best players in hockey history.

PATRICE BERGERON

1X STANLEY CUP (2011)

3X NHL ALL-STAR GAMES

2X WINTER OLYMPICS GOLD MEDAL

BORN
July 24, 1985
L'Ancienne-Lorette,
Quebec, Canada

SHOOTS
Right

POSITION
Center

34

Patrice Bergeron was picked 45th overall in the 2003 NHL Draft. When he first joined the Bruins, he wasn't the most powerful goal scorer, the fastest skater, or even the toughest player in his draft class.

He hadn't been the top scorer in his league, or even on his team. No one at the Bruins or the fans guessed that he would become one of the most important players in Bruins history.

Patrice earned a spot in the Bruins' lineup as an 18-year-old, jumping straight into the big leagues. But moving to Boston was not easy for him. He didn't know how to speak English; he only spoke French. But he worked hard, and soon, on October 18, 2003, he scored his first point against the Los Angeles Kings.

As he gained experience, the Bruins' general manager began to see something special in Patrice. He noticed his hard work, good sportsmanship, and leadership both on and off the ice.

So, in the 2005-06 season, Patrice played as the team's number one center. He led the Bruins in scoring that season, with a career-high of 31 goals and 73 points.

One of the unique things about Patrice was how he trained. He would copy the movements of the goalies. He practised reaching out with a glove hand or dropping down into a butterfly position.

People thought it was strange at first because Patrice wasn't a goalie. But he was trying to understand what the goalies were doing so he could figure out how to score against them.

In the 2013 playoffs, Patrice showed everyone just how tough he was. In Game 6 of the Stanley Cup finals against the Chicago Blackhawks, Patrice had a cracked rib. It hurt even when he walked, and he moved around like an old man. But he didn't even think about sitting out the game.

"The team needs me," he told himself. "This is a must-win game, and I have to be out there."

When the game started, the pain got worse and worse, but Patrice kept playing. Sadly, the Bruins lost the finals in a heartbreaker. But, Patrice became famous in the hockey world for showing his toughness and determination.

In 2021, at 35 years old, Patrice was named the 20th captain in Bruins history. As captain, he led the team with a spirit of hard work, respect, and selflessness.

On April 30, 2023, Patrice played his final game in a Bruins uniform. By then, he had scored 427 goals and earned 1,040 regular-season points over 19 seasons! He left behind an incredible legacy as one of the Bruins' all-time greatest players.

JOHNNY BUCYK

**2X STANLEY CUP
(1970, 1972)**

7X NHL ALL-STAR GAMES

**2X LADY BYNG MEMORIAL
TROPHY**

BORN
May 12, 1935
Edmonton, Alberta,
Canada

SHOOTS
Left

POSITION
Left Wing

Johnny "Chief" Bucyk was a left wing with incredible scoring power. He played 21 seasons for the Bruins, became the 12th captain in the team's history, and won two Stanley Cups.

Chief was part of a famous line known as the "Uke Line." This line was created in 1957 and included Chief, Bronco Horvath, and Vic Stasiuk. All three players had a Ukrainian background. They had played together before on a team called the Edmonton Flyers.

The "Uke Line" was a powerful offensive weapon for the Bruins over four seasons. They were one of the most exciting forward lines in hockey, playing together from 1957 to 1961.

They scored a total of 265 goals and earned 632 points, averaging 66 goals and 158 points per season. Their best year was 1959-1960 when they scored 84 goals and earned 200 points as a line.

Chief played most of his career at 220 pounds, making him one of the heaviest players on the ice. But he wasn't just big; he was also very skilled. He could deliver crushing hip checks, but he could also make smooth, precise plays. Despite his tough, physical style, he was known for being a clean and respectful player.

Chief became the captain of the Bruins for the 1966-67 season, and then again from 1973 to 1977. As captain, he set a high standard for his teammates. He expected them to train hard and give their best effort in every game. His leadership played a huge role in the Bruins' success during those years.

Chief was also known for his incredible playmaking. He often waited near the left post, where he could quickly score with his fast release and powerful backhand shot.

He had amazing passing skills too. He could send the puck through the tiniest gaps—between a defender's skates, under their stick, or over it. It was like he could thread a needle with the puck!

When Chief retired in 1978, he had earned 1,369 regular-season points with 556 goals and 813 assists. He still holds the record for the most assists by a left wing in NHL history. In 2017, he was voted one of the top 100 players of all time by the NHL.

ZDENO CHARA

1X STANLEY CUP (2011)

6X NHL ALL-STAR GAMES

1X JAMES NORRIS MEMORIAL TROPHY

BORN
18 March 1977
Trenčín, Czechoslovakia

SHOOTS
Left

POSITION
Defense

Playing against Zdeno Chara is like trying to get past a giant. At 6 feet 9 inches tall and weighing 250 pounds, he is the tallest player in NHL history! His huge, strong presence on the ice could make other players nervous. That's why he got the nickname "Big Z."

But Zdeno wasn't just a giant; he was a gentle giant. He played with the Bruins for 14 seasons, starting in 2006. When he joined, the team was rebuilding. They made him their captain right away, looking to Big Z for leadership.

Zdeno was known for being very serious about his training. He kept a dark blue folder filled with notes on every one of his workouts. He wrote down each exercise, the number of repetitions, and the weights he used. He was always working hard to get better.

As he got older, Zdeno wanted to keep up with the younger, faster players, so he started working with a skating coach. The coach taught him how to pivot more quickly when turning.

He also learned to skate with a lower stance to make himself faster. At first, it felt weird for Zdeno, but he kept practicing until he got it right.

Zdeno's discipline didn't stop on the ice. During flights, while his teammates played card games or watched movies, he would sit in the back and read. He loved non-fiction books that helped him become a better leader and person.

All of his hard work paid off when he led the Bruins to win the 2011 Stanley Cup against the Vancouver Canucks. It was a huge moment because it was the Bruins' first Stanley Cup win since 1972.

When Zdeno left the Bruins in 2020 to join the Washington Capitals, he left behind a lot of great memories.

Bruins fans will always remember his 2011 Stanley Cup win, his incredible hat trick against the Carolina Hurricanes in 2011, and the fact that he had the hardest shot in the NHL!

DAVID PASTRŇÁK

4X NHL ALL-STAR GAMES

1X NHL ALL-STAR GAME MVP

1X MAURICE "ROCKET" RICHARD TROPHY

BORN
25 May 1996
Havířov, Czech Republic

SHOOTS
Right

POSITION
Right Wing

David Pastrňák's hockey journey began with bus rides to a small rink in his hometown in the Czech Republic. His dad was a professional hockey player and coach, so David grew up around the game.

His dad put him on skates for the first time when he was only two-and-a-half. By the time he was three, David was already playing competitive hockey. When his dad passed away from cancer, David wanted to make his dad proud by becoming a great hockey player.

To chase his dream, David moved to Sweden to play in the second-best league there. He worked hard, improved a lot, and even led his team in points.

In 2014, the Boston Bruins drafted David as the 25th pick overall in the NHL Entry Draft. At the time, he had suffered a concussion, which caused many teams to pass on drafting him. But the Bruins saw his talent and decided he was too good to pass up, even though it was a bit risky.

When the Bruins called his name at the draft, David looked up at the sky. He could feel his dad was watching over him at that incredible moment.

Shortly after joining the team, David quickly became known as one of the league's top goal scorers. He was famous for his lightning-fast speed and accurate shooting. Even though he was just 19 years old, he became a player everyone had to watch out for in the NHL.

With each game-winning goal he scored, David rose to stardom. He became a fan favorite, and they affectionately nicknamed him "Pasta."

His third season was his breakout year, where he scored 34 goals and got 36 assists in just 70 games. He also found instant chemistry with Brad Marchand and Patrice Bergeron. They became known as the "Perfection Line."

At first, the coach wanted to keep David off the top line to spread out the offense. But when David, Brad, and Patrice played together, their chemistry was undeniable. They became one of the best forward lines in hockey history!

David's journey to the NHL is an inspiring story for young hockey players everywhere. He went from humble beginnings in a small rink to the bright lights of the NHL. It showed the world the power of hard work, determination, and believing in yourself.

BRAD MARCHAND

1X STANLEY CUP (2011)

2X NHL ALL-STAR GAMES

1X IIHF WORLD CHAMPIONSHIP GOLD MEDAL

BORN
May 11, 1988
Hammonds Plains,
Nova Scotia, Canada

SHOOTS
Left

POSITION
Left Wing

50

On the ice, Brad Marchand is known for his fierce competitive spirit mixed with a bit of anger. Even when he was a young hockey player, he had a reputation for being aggressive and getting into fights during games.

When Brad was young, he wasn't the best kid on his team. He also wasn't the tallest or the strongest. His friends were better players, and they were getting all the attention from the junior teams. Meanwhile, Brad struggled to get noticed.

One day, he realized that people started paying attention when he played rough against another kid on the other team. This style of play got him noticed by the junior teams, and later, it got him drafted by the Boston Bruins in 2009. Everyone saw him as a small-sized player who worked hard for the puck, always grinding it out on the ice.

After two seasons in the AHL, Brad got called up to the Bruins for the entire 2010–2011 season. From that moment on, everything changed for him.

At first, the team wanted him to play on the fourth line, a role that involves drawing penalties and killing them. It's not an easy or glamorous position, and it's definitely not for everyone. But for Brad, his hard work and toughness made him perfect for this job.

Brad's pesky style of play drew criticism from fans and opponents. Many NHL players even called him the "dirtiest player in the league."

But on April 2, 2011, he was awarded the Bruins' 7th Player Award, which is voted on by the fans. This award is given each year to the Bruins player who performs beyond expectations.

By the playoffs that year, Brad had moved up from the fourth line to the first line with Patrice Bergeron.

Over the seasons, Brad became an important part of the team. He was part of the legendary "Perfection Line" with Patrice Bergeron and David Pastrňák. He helped the Bruins win the Stanley Cup in 2011. At the same time, his on-ice behavior often got him into trouble with the NHL.

In recent seasons, Brad matured and changed the way he played. He started to move past his reputation as an agitator and focused more on his stats and being productive.

The Bruins noticed his growth. On September 20, 2023, Brad was named the captain of the Bruins. He became the 27th captain in the team's history.

CHAPTER THREE QUIZ

1. How old was Bobby Orr when he joined the Boston Bruins?

a. 17 years old

b. 18 years old

c. 19 years old

d. 20 years old

2. How many Hart Memorial trophies does Bobby Orr have?

a. 2

b. 3

c. 5

d. 8

3. What position did Bobby Orr play?

a. Defenseman

b. Goaltender

c. Center

d. Forward

4. Which team did the Bruins win against at the 1970 Stanley Cup Finals?

a. New York Rangers

b. Montreal Canadiens

c. Pittsburgh Penguins

d. St. Louis Blues

5. How many NHL All-Star games did Bobby Orr play in?

a. 7

b. 10

c. 14

d. 16

6. How many seasons did Ray Bourque play for the Boston Bruins?

a. 16 seasons

b. 18 seasons

c. 21 seasons

d. 23 seasons

7. Which season did Ray Bourque make his rookie debut for the Bruins?

a. 1976-77 season

b. 1979-80 season

c. 1983-84 season

d. 1988-89 season

8. How many Norris trophies does Ray Bourque have?

a. 4

b. 5

c. 7

d. 8

9. Which season was Ray Bourque made Bruins captain?

a. 1982

b. 1983

c. 1984

d. 1985

10. How many seasons was Ray Bourque the captain of the Bruins?

a. 12

b. 15

c. 17

d. 19

11. To which team was Ray Bourque traded in 2000?

a. Colorado Avalanche

b. New York Islanders

c. Washington Capitals

d. Carolina Hurricanes

12. How many NHL All-Star games did Ray Bourque play in?

a. 7

b. 10

c. 14

d. 19

13. What position did Phil Esposito play?

a. Defenseman

b. Goaltender

c. Center

d. Forward

14. Which year was Phil Esposito traded to the Bruins?

a. 1967

b. 1968

c. 1970

d. 1971

15. How many Art Ross trophies does Phil Esposito have?

a. 4

b. 5

c. 7

d. 8

16. How many NHL All-Star games did Phil Esposito play in?

a. 7

b. 10

c. 14

d. 16

17. Which team did Phil Esposito join in 1975?

a. New Jersey Devils

b. Dallas Stars

c. Los Angeles Kings

d. New York Rangers

18. In which year was Phil Esposito elected to the Hockey Hall of Fame?

a. 1980

b. 1982

c. 1984

d. 1986

19. In which year was Patrice Bergeron picked 45th overall in the NHL Draft?

a. 2002

b. 2003

c. 2004

d. 2005

20. Which team did Patrice Bergeron score his first point against?

a. Los Angeles Kings

b. Florida Panthers

c. Vegas Golden Knights

d. Vancouver Canucks

21. In which season was Patrice Bergeron chosen as the team's number one center?

a. 2004-05 season

b. 2005-06 season

c. 2006-07 season

d. 2007-08 season

22. How many NHL All-Star games did Patrice Bergeron play in?

a. 3

b. 7

c. 9

d. 10

23. How old was Patrice Bergeron when he was named the 20th captain in Bruins history?

a. 30 years old

b. 32 years old

c. 35 years old

d. 37 years old

24. What was Johnny Bucyk's nickname?

a. Uke

b. Ringo

c. Chief

d. Bucky

25. What is the name of the famous line that Johnny Bucyk was a part of?

a. Big Line

b. Uke Line

c. Forward Line

d. Bad Line

26. How many seasons did Johnny Bucyk play for the Boston Bruins?

a. 16 seasons

b. 18 seasons

c. 21 seasons

d. 23 seasons

27. In which year did Johnny Bucyk retire?

a. 1978

b. 1980

c. 1981

d. 1983

28. What was Zdeno Chara's nickname?

a. Giant

b. Big Z

c. Monster

d. The Tower

29. How many seasons did Zdeno Chara play for the Boston Bruins?

a. 14 seasons

b. 17 seasons

c. 20 seasons

d. 23 seasons

30. Which year was Zdeno Chara traded to the Bruins?

a. 2004

b. 2005

c. 2006

d. 2007

31. Which team did Zdeno Chara join after leaving the Boston Bruins?

a. San Jose Sharks

b. Washington Capitals

c. St. Louis Blues

d. Philadelphia Flyers

32. Which country is David Pastrňák from?

a. Germany

b. Sweden

c. Czech Republic

d. Poland

33. Which country did David Pastrňák move to play hockey before being drafted by the Boston Bruins?

a. Canada

b. Sweden

c. Russia

d. Italy

34. What position does David Pastrňák play?

a. Right Wing

b. Goaltender

c. Center

d. Forward

35. In which year did the Boston Bruins draft David Pastrňák as the 25th pick overall in the NHL Entry Draft?

a. 2012

b. 2013

c. 2014

d. 2015

36. What is David Pastrňák's nickname?

a. Pasta

b. Prodigy

c. Patriot

d. Powershot

37. What is the name of the famous line that David Pastrňák was a part of with Brad Marchand and Patrice Bergeron?

a. Power Line

b. Czech Mate Line

c. Tiger Line

d. Perfection Line

38. In which year was Brad Marchand drafted by the Boston Bruins?

a. 2009

b. 2010

c. 2012

d. 2014

39. How many seasons did Brad Marchand spend in the AHL before being called up by the Bruins?

a. 1

b. 2

c. 3

d. 4

40. What award did Brad Marchand win on April 2, 2011?

a. Elizabeth C. Dufresne Trophy

b. John P. Bucyk Award

c. Bruins' 7th Player Award

d. Eddie Shore Award

41. In which year was Brad Marchand named the captain of the Bruins?

a. 2020

b. 2021

c. 2022

d. 2023

Quiz Answers

1. 18 years old **2.** 3 Hart Memorial trophies **3.** Defenseman **4.** St. Louis Blues **5.** 7 NHL All-Star games **6.** 21 seasons **7.** 1979-80 season **8.** 5 Norris trophies **9.** 1985 **10.** 15 seasons **11.** Colorado Avalanche **12.** 19 NHL All-Star games **13.** Center **14.** 1967 **15.** 5 Art Ross trophies **16.** 10 NHL All-Star games **17.** New York Rangers **18.** 1984 **19.** 2003 NHL Draft **20.** Los Angeles Kings **21.** 2005-06 season **22.** 3 NHL All-Star games **23.** 35 years old **24.** Chief **25.** Uke Line **26.** 21 seasons **27.** 1978 **28.** Big Z **29.** 14 seasons **30.** 2006 **31.** Washington Capitals **32.** Czech Republic **33.** Sweden **34.** Right Wing **35.** 2014 **36.** Pasta **37.** Perfection Line **38.** 2009 **39.** 2 seasons **40.** Bruins' 7th Player Award **41.** 2023

CHAPTER FOUR

Coaches And Their Impact

Behind every great NHL team is a visionary Head Coach who inspires players and creates a winning culture. During the Bruins' long history, many legendary Head Coaches have guided the team through Stanley Cup finals and challenges from the bench.

Claude Julien is considered one of the greatest head coaches in Boston Bruins history. He coached the team from 2007 to 2017, and it became one of the most successful periods for the Bruins.

Claude is the winningest coach in the history of the team. His biggest moment came in 2011 when he led the Bruins to a thrilling Stanley Cup victory. That year, they defeated the

Vancouver Canucks in seven games. It was a huge celebration, as it took the Bruins 40 years to lift the Stanley Cup again!

During his 10 years as head coach, the Bruins only missed the playoffs twice. The team made the playoffs in each of his first seven seasons. On February 13, 2016, Claude Julien achieved a major milestone. He won his 500th NHL game as the Bruins defeated the Minnesota Wild 4–2.

In 2013, he once again led the Bruins to the Stanley Cup Finals. This time, they faced the Chicago Blackhawks. The Bruins fought hard, but they lost the series in six games. Even though they didn't win, Claude's coaching kept the team competitive and strong.

Claude Julien's time with the Bruins will always be remembered for his hard work, dedication, and for bringing the Stanley Cup back to Boston.

Another important head coach for the Bruins was Don Cherry. Don coached the team for five seasons, from 1974 to 1979. He made a big impact on the team, even though he never won a Stanley Cup.

When Don first joined the Bruins, the team had already won two Stanley Cups and finished in first place three times. But they were now without their superstars, Bobby Orr and Phil Esposito.

Don quickly became known for his loud, eccentric, and aggressive personality. He loved encouraging his players to play rough and physical hockey. He was even inspired by his dog, a feisty bull terrier! He added tough players, known as enforcers and grinders, to the team. This new style made the Bruins known as the "Big Bad Bruins."

Thanks to this change, the Bruins continued to be one of the NHL's best teams. They won the Adams Division title for four straight seasons. Don was named NHL Coach of the Year, winning the Jack Adams Award in 1975.

But things didn't always go perfectly for Don. The Bruins reached the Stanley Cup Finals twice, in 1977 and 1978. But, they lost both times to their arch-rivals, the Montreal Canadiens.

Then, in 1979, the Bruins lost to the Canadiens again in the semi-final playoff series. After that, the team decided it was time for a change and let Don go.

Despite not winning the Stanley Cup, Don Cherry has left a lasting mark on the Bruins' history.

CHAPTER FOUR QUIZ

1. From which year to which year did Claude Julien coach the Boston Bruins?

a. 2000-2015

b. 2007-2017

c. 1991-1998

d. 2003-2019

2. How many Stanley Cups did Claude Julien win with the Bruins?

a. 1

b. 2

c. 3

d. 4

3. In which year did Claude Julien win his Stanley Cup with the Bruins?

a. 2000

b. 2005

c. 2008

d. 2011

4. In which year did Don Cherry become the head coach of the Bruins?

a. 1958

b. 1960

c. 1967

d. 1974

5. In which year did Don Cherry win his Jack Adams Award?

a. 1960

b. 1966

c. 1967

d. 1975

6. Which team did the Bruins lose to in the Stanley Cup Finals in both 1977 and 1978?

a. Montreal Canadiens

b. Buffalo Sabres

c. Florida Panthers

d. Ottawa Senators

Quiz Answers

1. 2007-2017 **2.** 1 Stanley Cup **3.** 2011 **4.** 1974 **5.** 1975 **6.** Montreal Canadiens

CHAPTER FIVE

Memorable Moments in Bruins' History

The Boston Bruins have had some amazing moments that fans will never forget.

From winning the Bruins' first Stanley Cup in 1929 to special moments like the 2013 playoffs comeback, here are five exciting and unforgettable moments in Bruins history.

FIRST STANLEY CUP VICTORY (1929)

The 1929 Stanley Cup championship is one of the greatest moments in Boston Bruins history. It was the team's first-ever Stanley Cup win, just five years after joining the NHL!

"Can you believe it, boys? We're in the Stanley Cup Final!" Coach Art Ross exclaimed in the locker room. "We've come a long way in just five years, Coach," a player replied, grinning.

The Bruins first had to defeat the Montreal Canadiens in the semifinals. Then, in the Stanley Cup Final, they faced the defending champions, the New York Rangers. The Rangers were a strong team, having won the Cup in 1928.

The game was especially exciting because of two players. It was a battle between the Bruins' goalie Cecil "Tiny" Thompson and the Rangers' forward Paul Thompson.

These two were brothers, and it was the first time in Stanley Cup Finals history that brothers faced each other as a goalie and a forward.

"Hey Tiny," Paul called out during warm-ups, "no hard feelings when I score on you, right?" Tiny laughed, "In your dreams, little brother. You're not getting anything past me!"

In Game 1, the Bruins won 2-0, with Tiny Thompson making an incredible shutout performance, proving just how good he was.

Then, the series moved to New York's Madison Square Garden for Game 2. The Rangers were undefeated and hadn't let in a single goal during the 1929 playoffs. But Bruins' right-winger Harry 'Pee Wee' Oliver ended that streak with a goal at 14:01 of the second period.

"Nice shot, Pee Wee!" his teammates cheered as Oliver skated back to the bench.

The Bruins went on to win the game 2-1, securing their first-ever Stanley Cup victory.

As the final buzzer sounded, the Bruins erupted in celebration. The 1929 Stanley Cup win was a huge turning point for the Boston Bruins. It also set the stage for American teams to succeed in a league that had been dominated by Canadian teams up until that point.

BREAKING THE NHL COLOR LINE (1958)

Growing up in Fredericton, Willie O'Ree's family was one of the only two black families in the city. Hockey was a huge sport in Canada, and young boys and girls grew up playing the game.

Like his other friends in school, Willie also fell in love with hockey. Since his family did not have a TV, he would listen to Hockey Night in Canada on the radio. He would even skate to school when the weather allowed.

He dreamed of playing professional hockey one day, like his idol Maurice Richard. But, unlike his friends, there was no other hockey player who looked like him in the NHL.

But, that did not stop Willie from loving the sport. When he was out skating on the rinks, he did not experience racism. The other boys treated him equally.

As he grew older, Willie became a very good hockey player. He was playing minor league hockey with the Quebec Aces when he had the opportunity to play for the Boston Bruins. Playing in the NHL went from being a dream to finally becoming a reality.

On January 18, 1958, Willie played his first NHL game against the Montreal Canadiens. He became the first black player in league history.

Although he was finally living his dream, it was not always easy for him.

While his hockey teammates were kind and welcoming, the players and fans from the other teams were mean to him. They would call him racist names and treat him badly. Being the only Black player in the NHL made him a target.

In one game during the 1960–61 season, a Chicago Black Hawks player taunted Willie and even hurt him intentionally. But Willie would not let anyone stop his determination of being an NHL hockey player.

After his time playing for the Bruins, he played 14 more years across Canadian and American leagues. Willie finally retired in 1979.

Because of his courage and determination, Willie became a trailblazer for diversity in hockey. He paved the way for Black players like Blake Bolden to become the first Black player in the National Women's Hockey League. Another Black player, Jarome Iginla, became a Hall of Famer.

Today, players of all races can dream of playing in the NHL.

2013 PLAYOFFS MIRACLE COMBACK

Every once in a while in sports, something happens that seems impossible. Can't. Shouldn't. The 2013 Game 7 victory over the Toronto Maple Leafs is one of those moments.

The Bruins' incredible comeback in Game 7 is remembered as one of the greatest comebacks in NHL playoff history.

On May 13, 2013, the Bruins faced the Toronto Maple Leafs. It was Game 7 of the Eastern Conference Quarter-Finals. The Bruins had jumped to a 3-1 series lead, but then lost Games 5 and 6. With the series tied at 3-3, both teams felt the pressure to win this decisive Game 7.

The game didn't start well for the Bruins. The Leafs took a big 4-1 lead halfway through the third period. They were quick with their relentless attacks.

With just over 10 minutes left, it seemed like the Bruins had almost no chance to win. The home crowd was starting to feel disappointed.

"Come on, guys, we can't give up now," Patrice Bergeron urged his teammates on the bench. "We've come too far to go out like this."

But then, something amazing happened. With 10 minutes and 42 seconds left, Nathan Horton scored a goal to make it 4-2! The Bruins were still down by two goals, but this goal gave them a spark of hope.

"That's what I'm talking about!" Horton shouted as he skated back to the bench. "We're not done yet!"

The team felt energized by Horton's goal and began to play even harder, giving everything they had. Their physical play and aggressive forechecking began to wear down the Leafs.

The Bruins decided to pull their goalie, Tuukka Rask, for an extra attacker. They were hoping it would help them score. The decision worked perfectly as Milan Lucic scored off a rebound to make it 4-3!

"Keep pushing!" Lucic yelled to his teammates.

The tension in TD Garden was electric, and suddenly, the comeback seemed possible.

With less than a minute left, the Bruins kept pushing hard against the Leafs' defense. Brad Marchand was crucial in these final moments, helping the Bruins keep the puck in the Leafs' zone.

"Marchy, over here!" Bergeron called out, positioning himself near the net.

With only 51 seconds remaining, Patrice Bergeron spotted a loose puck in front of the net. After a scramble with several blocked shots, he managed to shoot it past the goalie, tying the game at 4-4! The crowd went wild, and the Maple Leafs were stunned.

Just over six minutes into overtime, Bergeron got hold of another loose puck. He took a quick wrist shot through a crowd of players, and it slipped past the goalie! The Bruins won 5-4, completing one of the most amazing comebacks in NHL history.

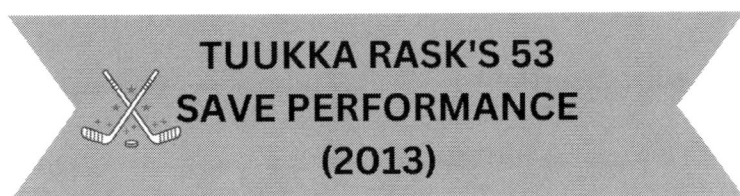

TUUKKA RASK'S 53 SAVE PERFORMANCE (2013)

Tuukka Rask was a Finnish goalie who played for the Bruins from 2007 to 2022. He was known for his amazing positioning and acrobatic saves.

On June 5, 2013, the Bruins were playing against the Pittsburgh Penguins. It was Game 3 of the Eastern Conference Finals. The Bruins already had a 2-0 lead in the series after winning Games 1 and 2.

The Penguins were desperate to turn things around. They came out with an aggressive plan, firing shot after shot at Tuukka right from the start. It seemed like he barely had a moment to breathe before another puck was heading his way!

But no matter how hard the Penguins tried, Tuukka kept stopping their relentless attack with his incredible saves. He stayed calm under pressure, frustrating the Penguins' star players again and again. By the end of regulation time, Tuukka had already made 45 saves, but the game was still tied 1-1.

"How are you feeling, Tuukka?" the goalie coach asked during the intermission.

Tuukka grinned, despite his exhaustion. "Like I could do this all night if I have to."

As the game went into overtime, both teams knew that one mistake could cost them everything. Everyone was exhausted, but Tuukka continued his incredible performance. The Penguins kept shooting, trying everything to score, but he wouldn't let anything get past him.

Finally, in the second overtime, Patrice Bergeron scored the game-winning goal!

Patrice Bergeron's goal was the moment that sealed the win. But, it was Tuukka's heroic performance in net that was the real story of the game.

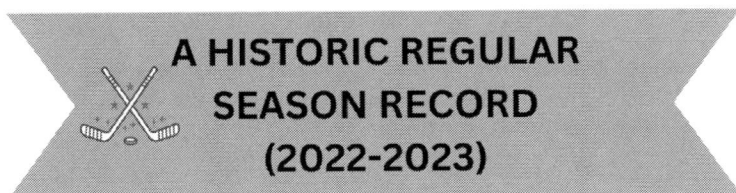

A HISTORIC REGULAR SEASON RECORD (2022-2023)

David Pastrňák took a moment to look around the arena at TD Garden. He had played over 260 games here, but today felt different. Today, the Bruins set a new league record with their 12th consecutive home win to start the season!

With first-year head coach Jim Montgomery leading them, the Bruins dominated the league from the very start. They began the 2022-23 season with a bang, winning eight of their nine games in October.

Many people were surprised by the Bruins' success. The team wasn't seen as a favorite this season. Some key players, like Brad Marchand and Charlie McAvoy, were out with injuries. But the Bruins quickly showed everyone that they were still dreaming of the Stanley Cup.

Coach Jim Montgomery brought in a new, more aggressive style of play. He wanted the team to play fast, stay on the attack, and fight hard for the puck. His approach helped the Bruins create more scoring chances and score more goals.

David Pastrňák was one of the standout players that season. He scored several hat tricks and even reached his 60th goal of the season on April 9, 2023.

Thanks to a new coach and Pastrňák's amazing performance, the Bruins had several long winning streaks throughout the season.

Sadly, the Bruins had a heartbreaking end in the 2023 Stanley Cup Playoffs. Still, the 2022-2023 season will always be remembered as one of the greatest in NHL history. They broke records for the most wins (65 wins) and the most points (135 points) in a single regular season!

CHAPTER FIVE QUIZ

1. What was the final score of the 1929 Stanley Cup series?

a. 2-1

b. 3-1

c. 3-2

d. 4-1

2. Who was the coach who led the Bruins to victory in the 1929 Stanley Cup Final?

a. Claude Julien

b. Art Ross

c. Bruce Cassidy

d. Harry Sinden

3. In which year did Willie O'Ree play his first NHL game?

a. 1950

b. 1955

c. 1958

d. 1963

4. Which team did Willie O'Ree face in his NHL debut?

a. Los Angeles Kings

b. Edmonton Oilers

c. Pittsburgh Penguins

d. Montreal Canadiens

5. Which player scored the winning goal in Game 7 of the Eastern Conference Quarter-Finals?

a. Nathan Horton

b. Milan Lucic

c. Patrice Bergeron

d. Brad Marchand

6. How many saves did Tuukka Rask make in Game 3 of the Eastern Conference Finals?

a. 50 saves

b. 53 saves

c. 57 saves

d. 59 saves

7. How many games did the Bruins win during the 2022-2023 season?

a. 60 wins

b. 63 wins

c. 65 wins

d. 70 wins

Quiz Answers

1. 2-1 **2.** Art Ross **3.** 1958 **4.** Montreal Canadiens **5.** Patrice Bergeron **6.** 53 saves **7.** 65 wins

CHAPTER SIX

Fun Facts and Trivia: Did You Know, Nicknames, And Pop Culture

The team's mascot is the Blades the Bruin. Blades the Bruin is a cute but fierce brown bear that was first introduced in 1999.

The Boston Bruins have retired the jersey numbers of eleven legendary players, including 4 (Bobby Orr), 7 (Phil Esposito), and 8 (Cam Neely).

The Bruins are the only Original Six team that have not retired the uniform number 1.

When the Bruins won the Stanley Cup in 1941, Pat McReavy's name was misspelled in the engraving. The engraver spelled his name as Pat McCeavy.

Ray Bourque was Boston Bruins' longest-serving captain. He played 21 seasons with the Bruins. He is also the all-time leader in points, assists, and games played by a Bruins player.

Former Bruins goaltender Tim Thomas holds the all-time record for the highest saves recorded in a season. He ended the 2010/11 season with a .938 save record. This performance helped the Bruins win their first Stanley Cup in nearly 40 years.

The first owner of the Bruins was Charles Francis Adams. He was a wealthy grocery chain tycoon from Vermont. Charles was an avid hockey fan and wanted to bring professional hockey to the United States. He remained president of the club until 1936, before passing over the reins to his son Weston.

The Bruins' colors were originally brown and gold. They wore brown uniforms in their first season, but switched to a white uniform with alternating brown and gold stripes the next season.

David Pastrňák is known by the nickname "Pasta." In 2021, he partnered with Stop & Shop to release his own limited-edition penne pasta. It was priced at 88 cents to honor his jersey number. All the proceeds went to pediatric cancer research.

The Boston Bruins' goal song is "Kernkraft 400" by German techno musician Zombie Nation. It is played after every goal scored by the Bruins.

For 8 years, Zdeno Chara held the record for the hardest shot in NHL history. The 6-foot-9 Boston Bruins captain blasted the puck 108.8 mph into the open net. In 2020, this record was broken by Martin Frk with a 109.2 mph shot.

The Bruins were the first NHL team to feature an African-American player. In 1958, the Boston Bruins made history by becoming the first NHL team to include Willie O'Ree, an African-American player. This broke barriers and paved the way for greater diversity in hockey.

Brad Marchand does not watch many movies, but his favorite is the 2000 film The Patriot. He also enjoys watching Teenage Mutant Ninja Turtles, and his favorite Ninja Turtle is Leonardo.

Some of the Boston Bruins' famous fans include Steve Carell, John Krasinski, Ben Affleck, and Adam Sandler.

HERE ARE MORE QUESTIONS TO TEST YOUR KNOWLEDGE OF THE BRUINS!

1. Who was the first Boston Bruins player to win the Hart Trophy as the NHL's Most Valuable Player?

a. Eddie Shore

b. Bobby Orr

c. Milt Schmidt

d. Ray Bourque

2. Which team did the Bruins defeat to win the 2011 Stanley Cup?

a. Chicago Blackhawks

b. St. Louis Blues

c. Vancouver Canucks

d. Detroit Red Wings

3. Who was the Boston Bruins' captain before Brad Marchand?

a. Patrice Bergeron

b. Zdeno Chara

c. Joe Thornton

d. Ray Bourque

4. Who was the first Boston Bruins player to have his number retired?

a. Lionel Hitchman

b. Bobby Orr

c. Eddie Shore

d. Milt Schmidt

5. Which player holds the Boston Bruins' record for the most assists in a single season?

a. Bobby Orr

b. Ray Bourque

c. Phil Esposito

d. Rick Middleton

6. Who was the first player in Bruins history to score 50 goals in a single season?

a. Cam Neely

b. Johnny Bucyk

c. Phil Esposito

d. Bobby Orr

7. Who was the first Eastern European-born player to captain the Boston Bruins?

a. Ray Bourque

b. Zdeno Chara

c. Marco Sturm

d. David Krejci

8. What is the longest point streak by a Bruins player in a single season?

a. 19 points

b. 22 points

c. 26 points

d. 30 points

9. Which player was known as "The Little Ball of Hate" while playing for the Bruins?

a. Cam Neely

b. Terry O'Reilly

c. Eddie Shore

d. Brad Marchand

10. What is the name of the Boston Bruins' American Hockey League (AHL) affiliate?

a. Providence Bruins

b. Worcester IceCats

c. Springfield Thunderbirds

d. Maine Mariners

11. Who was the Bruins' head coach at the start of the 2023-2024 NHL season?

a. Bruce Cassidy

b. Claude Julien

c. Jim Montgomery

d. Don Sweeney

12. What big achievement did the Bruins reach in the 2022-2023 season about their number of wins?

a. Most wins in a regular season

b. Most consecutive wins

c. Most wins in a playoff series

d. Most wins in franchise history

13. Which Boston Bruins rookie made his NHL debut in the 2023-2024 season?

a. Fabian Lysell

b. Jack Studnicka

c. Urho Vaakanainen

d. Johnny Beecher

ABOUT THE AUTHOR

John Stevenson is a Michigan-based author of children's sports books. He is the father of two children, James and Tracy. When not writing new books, John can be found playing sports with his family or going on road trips. Through his books, John hopes to empower young readers and spark their imagination.

ENJOYED THE BOOK?

I'd really appreciate it if you could leave a review on Amazon. The number of reviews a book receives helps more people discover it. Even a short review can make a big difference, allowing me to keep doing what I love. Thank you in advance!

Trivia Answers

1. Eddie Shore **2.** Vancouver Canucks **3.** Patrice Bergeron **4.** Lionel Hitchman **5.** Bobby Orr **6.** Phil Esposito **7.** Zdeno Chara **8.** 22 points **9.** Brad Marchand **10.** Providence Bruins **11.** Jim Montgomery **12.** Most wins in a regular season **13.** Johnny Beecher

Made in the USA
Columbia, SC
15 February 2025